STEP THREE

Giving Up
the Game

First published May, 1982

Printed in the United States of America.

The following is an adaptation of one of the Twelve Steps in the program of Overeaters Anonymous. It is one person's interpretation and does not speak for the O.A. organization.

Where it's at

Step Three begins a process of active commitment to the Overeaters Anonymous program. Whereas we were in a passive position for Steps One and Two — admitting powerlessness and acknowledging a Higher Power — in Step Three we make a positive, active decision which will affect every area of life. It is a decision which we renew on a daily basis.

For some of us, making the decision seems like jumping off the edge of a cliff. We would probably never be willing to take this "leap of faith" if the pain of hanging on to our old ways had not become greater than the fear of letting go.

"Trust God to take care of my life? How do I know He will? I'm not even sure there is a God." Trusting a Higher Power may be very hard for you to do. But if you are truly desperate, you may be willing to try it anyway, on the recommendation of people who can vouch for the fact that it has worked for them. You can start with just a tiny bit of willingness to trust. As you take the risk and as you see that it makes a positive difference in your life, your level of trust rises.

Remember, this is a "one day at a time" program. What is clearly "impossible for the rest of my life" can be done just for today. *Today* I can take Step Three. I can decide to turn my will and my life over to the care of God as I understand Him just for today. I don't have to worry about tomorrow. I may get run over by a bus tomorrow. Or I may never make it through tonight. All I have is now, today. If I can trust providence to take care of me now, chances are that I will also be able to trust tomorrow, and the next day, one day at a time.

As compulsive people, we grasp for certainty. We think we would like to have everything nailed down, know where we're going, where we're going to be ten years from now, and especially, know that everything will be fine and dandy. Part of our irrational overeating is undoubtedly an attempt to find certainty and assurance in food. But the only solid result of overeating is fat!

Deciding to trust God instead of food is a one hundred eighty degree turnaround in attitude. We are changing from a material orientation to a spiritual one. And we may fear that if the bottom falls out of this rather shaky Higher Power business, we will be left exposed and defenseless.

What is the alternative? We can continue to try to manage our own lives and continue searching for a way to stop overeating. We can continue to trust food, money, intelligence, sex, good business connections, family, friends, a psychiatrist, etc., to solve our problems and make us happy. Not that all of these things aren't important and helpful — they are. But are they filling the emptiness? Has trying to run our own lives produced inner peace? Can we stop overeating without a Power greater than ourselves?

If after an honest evaluation we conclude that we have made rather a mess of things by ourselves, Step Three begins to look like a practical move to make. In reality, turning our will and our lives over to God means that we are finally establishing them on a firm foundation. What was shaky was our own willfulness. Surrendering self-will and letting a Higher Power run our lives is

the core of the program which promises us freedom from
compulsive overeating.

Turning it over

"It's out of control, H.P. Everything. The food, the
interpersonal relationships, the work — everything. You'll
have to take over. I'm tired. I can't do anything right. I'm scared.
I'm confused. I should have stayed in bed this morning. I'll never
get through the day. Help!"

So it goes. Each day we ask for help, we strengthen our
conscious commitment to spiritual growth. Each time we try it,
the answers become more clear. One day at a time, we allow our
self-will to conform more closely to God's will.

Not ready for that kind of commitment? Are you ready
to make a beginning? Are you willing to go along with the idea
that whatever plan a Higher Power has for your life, it probably
does not include compulsive overeating?

If that is the case, doesn't it seem reasonable that God will
make available to you the strength to resist the first
compulsive bite, as long as you are sincerely trying to follow
His plan for your life?

We grow up with the idea that *we* should make the plans,
know where we are going, be sure that our desires are satisfied,
self-actualized. "What do I want to do with my life?" As long
as the accent is on I, me, mine, we are limiting our potential for
growth. We discover that we want one thing today and another

tomorrow and something else the day after. Self-actualizing with only our own limited power may not get us very far.

In fact, most of us find that living according to the capricious dictates of self-will leads to messed up relationships with other people and slavery to out-of-control appetites. We get bogged down in false dependencies — in the case of the compulsive overeater, excess food. Fear and anxiety increase.

Then what happens? Either we continue down the path of addiction — a circular path, since overeating makes us feel bad and then we eat more to feel better — or we get outside help.

When we decide that using excess food to reduce fear and anxiety does not work and is slowly destroying us, we have to find another way of coping with these feelings. The Twelve Step program shows us how to live without using excess food as a crutch. We turn the eating problem over to a Higher Power, since we cannot solve it ourselves. And, we turn over all of the other aspects of our lives, too, since we have come to believe that God can do a better job of managing and directing them than we can.

One day at a time

Living the Third Step means learning how to live one day at a time. When we are in tune with a Higher Power, we are living in the present instead of fretting over the past or fantasizing about the future. God is now. He gives us strength and power for what actually is happening right this minute. When we try to rewrite what happened a long time ago or when we worry about what might happen tomorrow and the next day, we lose touch with our source of strength. Wandering around in a head trip makes it easy to get lost.

There is just no way to know what tomorrow will bring. The best way to prepare for whatever will arrive is to maintain spiritual contact today. And the amazing thing is that when we stay plugged in to a Higher Power today, whatever comes up tomorrow turns out to be okay. Often it's even better than okay — a lot better.

It stands to reason that a Higher Power has access to "information" which you and I do not have. If we insist on operating only according to our limited vision, we restrict ourselves. Why limit our options? Turning our lives over to the care of the God of our understanding frees us from our own limitations. If we are listening now, one day at a time, to inner promptings, we become more spontaneous and creative. The pieces begin to fall into place. Situations that seemed impossible begin to untangle. We get the strength and the insight to deal with them on a daily basis.

One day at a time, one meal at a time. For the compulsive overeater, nothing is more important than staying in the here and now. I cannot conceive of being abstinent for the rest of my life, but with God's help and support of the group I can be abstinent just for today. I can abstain from this meal to the next. I have a food plan for today, and I will not worry about being hungry tomorrow or bingeing tomorrow. If I feel hungry this afternoon, I know that I will survive until dinner. After dinner, it is not likely that I will die of starvation before morning.

I believe that it is not God's will for me to overeat, and so I do today what is necessary to insure that I will not take the first compulsive bite. I know what I will eat for breakfast, lunch, and dinner. I make phone calls to friends in the program, go to meetings, read the literature, spend time keeping in touch with my Higher Power. I remember the how of the program: honesty, openmindedness, willingness. By doing this today, one day at a time, I can trust that the God who takes care of me today will also take care of me tomorrow.

Rebellion

I trust, but at the same time I rebell — rebell against writing down a food plan, rebell against calling it in to a sponsor, rebell against following it, rebell against letting God manage my life. Whatever it is, I want to do it my way. I want what I want when I want it — *now,* if not yesterday.

Overeating is a classic form of rebellion. Ever since Eve ate the apple, forbidden fruit has symbolized temptation. As soon as you try to go on a diet, everything that is not on it becomes much more desirable than before. That is one reason why diets do not work for compulsive overeaters. For us, a diet is definitely not enough.

Writing down a food plan can also generate rebellion. It is as though inside many of us there is a streak of obstinate perversity that drives us in an opposite direction where we know we should be going. We refuse to be told what to do. Even when we tell *ourselves* what to do with regard to food and three meals a day, we can react in the same way we did as children when parents tried to exercise control.

We become split personalities, at war with ourselves. One side is saying, "No, don't take the first compulsive bite," but another voice is screaming against the restraint and is determined to indulge at any cost. "You've had your measured meal and that's enough/I want more." "Don't blow it/Just a little taste won't hurt." "Stop eating/I'll do what I jolly well please and nobody can stop me."

The compulsion is baffling and cunning. It deludes us into thinking that this time we can get away with a little extra. "What am I, a robot or something? I don't need to weigh and measure all the time. I can exercise some judgment and be a little flexible today. I'll make up for it tomorrow." Then the little extra bite takes over and becomes a binge.

Self-will rebels at the idea of being directed by a Higher Power. It rebells against the existence of anything greater than itself. Self-will and appetite are closely connected. They line themselves up against the voices of reason and experience.

We can continue to rebell and continue down the path of self-destruction. We can continue to live lives of quiet desperation. We can follow our compulsion into insanity and/or death. As free agents, we can choose. Nobody, least of all God, is forcing us to surrender our will and our lives.

What is inevitable is that the illness of compulsive overeating will get worse if not arrested. Rebelling against the inevitable takes a great deal of energy, to say nothing of wasted time. How far each of us has to go before hitting bottom is variable, depending on individual factors. Sometimes bottom is a slow death from obesity-related diseases; sometimes it is sudden death due to cardiac arrest or esophageal rupture.

Fortunately, many of us can hit a "higher bottom" at an early stage of the illness by realizing where we are headed. When we get the insight as to where self-will is leading us, by the grace of God the wind goes out of our rebellious sails, and we run up the white flag of surrender.

Moment of decision

Once convinced that our self-will will eventually destroy us, we make the "decision to turn our will and our lives over to the care of God as we understood Him." In the words of the "Big Book"* of Alcoholics Anonymous, "We had to quit playing God. It didn't work." What happens when we take Step Three and make this decision is that we now have "a new Employer" and indeed feel "reborn." From now on, we know that a Higher Power is running the show, and we can relax. Playing God is hard work; maintaining the illusion of control involves tremendous fear and anxiety. It is a great relief to be able to give up the game.

You may want to take Step Three with your sponsor or someone else who is close to you. The following prayer is suggested on page 63 of the "Big Book." (Remember, this is to the God of *your understanding*.)

"God, I offer myself to Thee — to build with me and to do with me as Thou wilt. Relieve me of the bondage of self, that I may better do Thy will. Take away my difficulties, that victory over them may bear witness to those I would help, of Thy Power, Thy Love, and Thy Way of Life. May I do Thy Will always!"

If you don't like that prayer, don't say it. Everything in the

---

* *Alcoholics Anonymous,* published by A.A. World Services, New York, NY. Available through Hazelden Educational Materials.

11

program is merely suggested as an example of what has worked for others. You do not need to say any formal prayer. Making the Step Three decision can happen on a very deep, intuitive level without words. In a flash, you can decide to change from being ego-directed to being spiritually prompted. You may find, however, that consciously verbalizing the decision nails down the change in attitude. Then, when you are emotionally upset and things are getting out of hand, you can remind yourself of the concrete decision you have made to let a Higher Power run the show.

Step Three simplifies life considerably. It means that whatever the circumstances, our main intent is to know God's will for us and do it. Everything else will take care of itself.

Freedom

It is a paradox that the harder we try to find freedom and pleasure through indulging our wants, the more enslaved and unhappy we become. The longer we work this program, the more firmly convinced we are that trying to go against God's will is at the root of our dissatisfaction and frustration. To be hooked on oneself is perhaps the worst addiction of all! Working through substance addiction — whether it be alcohol abuse, drug abuse, or food abuse — brings all of us into a confrontation with self-centeredness.

Freedom from "the bondage of self" is what we are asking for in Step Three and what the program promises us.

Self-centeredness has driven us to the wall. We have tried to make ourselves happy by every conceivable means and find that the harder we try, the more miserable we become. One minute we think we will be happy if we can just be thin; the next minute, all we want is a pizza. A little while later, more money appears to be the solution to every problem. Then more love, more sex, more power. The list goes on and on.

In order to make ourselves happy, we try to control not only our own lives but everyone else's too — especially the lives of those we love. We think we know best. We have the mistaken idea that power and control will give us freedom, when in fact the effort to hang on makes us fearful and anxious. Trying to manipulate others to do what we want them to do is wasted energy and destroys our own spontaneity.

The only way to be free is to go along with the Power that runs the universe. Fighting God's will for us is a losing battle. When my will is harmony with the will of this Higher Power, I am free to be who I really am and do what I am supposed to do. I do not have to work out elaborate strategies to try to make things go my way. I do not have to worry about imminent disaster. Whatever happens will be right when I am sincerely trying to know and do God's will.

Freedom from self-will run riot includes freedom from compulsive overeating. The compulsion may not be lifted immediately upon taking the Third Step, but we are laying the groundwork that is crucial to maintaining abstinence. On the other hand, the compulsion may be lifted *before* we take the Third Step. This thing we call abstinence is a gift which is given to us daily, and it is dependent on our spiritual condition. Turning over our lives to a spiritual Power one day at a time will eventually give us the strength to stop eating compulsively.

What we sought in excess food was not to be found there. We were not satisfied; we wanted something more. Getting into the program and beginning to work the Steps gives us glimpses of a spiritual life which is qualitatively different from the way we were living before. This is not something more, not something added on to everything else we have. It is something entirely new, and it satisfies our hunger in a way that more never did.

Abstinence alone is not enough. We need to live *for* something. Through the program, we learn to live by and for a Power greater than ourselves. This brings us the satisfaction, peace, and love that we lacked, and so we no longer need to overeat.

Sound impossible? Wishful thinking? Try it. If you do not like the new life, your former misery will be refunded.

Freedom from the bondage of self eventually brings freedom from craving and freedom from fear. That is what results when we allow a Higher Power to run the show.

Of course, all of this does not happen immediately. Spiritual growth may be slow, but it is solid. As we look back on our lives, we see that God gives us what we need when we are ready for it. His timetable may surprise us, and we may not think we want all of what comes our way. We may get impatient and try to take back control. Then we are no longer free. We get entangled in the same old snarl of self-will.

But once having tasted the freedom that comes with surrender, we are never the same. We do not want to go back to the old life of rebellious indulgence. We've glimpsed the light at the end of the tunnel, and we are being pulled forward, drawn toward that light in spite of doubts and reservations that may still linger. The doubts will gradually fade as we experience the trust and freedom that we gain from surrendering to a Higher Power.

A commitment to abstinence

". . . deep down in every man, woman, and child is the fundamental idea of God," says the "Big Book" of A.A. We can find the "Great Reality deep down within us." When we find it, our entire attitude toward life is changed, and the miracle of healing can occur.

Making the decision to trust God with our lives — the small events as well as the big ones — opens the way to a fuller understanding of this "Great Reality" within us. When we make a Third Step commitment, we open the channels to God's power.

We become convinced on a gut level that compulsive overeating is contrary to God's will for our lives and, indeed, prevents us from living according to his direction. Therefore, turning our will and our lives over to God's care involves a commitment to abstinence as the will of our Higher Power.

Abstinence is something we practice regardless of how we feel. No matter how down or how great we feel, or even if we don't feel anything at all, we can maintain abstinence. The strength to do it comes from a Higher Power, and abstinence is ours to enjoy as long as we stay plugged into that source of strength. We do not even have to enjoy it, but if we think back to when we were bingeing and the misery we experienced then, enjoyment is a mild way to describe the new state.

We all know what happens if we lose abstinence. Food then takes the place of God, and the craving for more controls our lives. Energy and enthusiasm dissolve, each day becomes a chore, and chaos returns. If we let go of abstinence, we can never be sure when or if we will get it back again. What first compulsive bite is worth the wreckage?

Being committed to abstinence means that it has priority. For a compulsive overeater, no other consideration is more important. In times of trouble and in times of joy, our survival depends on remembering that we are compulsive overeaters and that abstinence comes first. To take the illness lightly or to think that we can get away with some cheating here and there is to forget that it is a progressive disease. Even after a long period of abstinence, if we return to compulsive overeating, we find that our binges are worse and the insanity is greater.

Committing ourselves to abstinence also means that we accept whatever discomfort and/or inconvenience may go along with it. We may have periods of hunger, depression, boredom, anxiety. We will undoubtedly have to face painful feelings that we formerly buried under a mountain of excess food. We may have to make special arrangements to insure that the food on our plan will be available when we need it. We become willing to go to any length in order to recover.

Food can no longer be an option when we are feeling bad or at loose ends. What do you turn to instead? O.A. gives us a support group. There are people to call and there is literature to read. We learn, moreover, that nothing insures our own abstinence better than working with and being of service to other compulsive overeaters.

We can turn to the group and we can turn to a Higher Power, letting go of our problems and praying for strength to carry our His will for our lives. We can be willing to hurt for a while as a small price to pay for recovery.

It is habit that lures us back into the old ways and tempts us to self-destruct. Once upon a time, compulsive overeating was fun,

16

and we would like to recapture that pleasure. We need to remember that the fun part is over and that from now on the first compulsive bite will always bring pain.

When the pain of overeating is worse than the pain of abstaining, we are on the way to recovery. Abstinence may not be much fun, but it is infinitely preferable to ever-worsening binges. Since most of us find that we cannot abstain without the help of a Higher Power, the commitment to abstinence insures that we are going to grow in our relationship to the God of our understanding. We have to ask for the strength to be abstinent on a daily basis, sometimes much more often. This keeps us in contact with a spiritual Power and keeps us growing.

Taking it back

Okay, so you took Step Three, you got your abstinence, everything was going fine for a few days, weeks, months, perhaps even years. Then something happened. Maybe you forgot that you were a compulsive overeater. Maybe you let some part of your life become more important than maintaining abstinence. Maybe you forgot about your Higher Power.

At any rate, you lost your abstinence and you took back not only the eating problem but also the living problem. It could be that it happened the other way around — you tried to take back control of other areas of your life such as sex, money, work, etc., and before long you discovered that your abstinence was slipping.

Basically it all boils down to whether we are letting God have control or whether we are trying to manage everything ourselves. We have proved over and over again that the first way works and the second does not.

So why do we take back all the problems? Before coming down too hard on ourselves, it's good to remember that we expect progress, not perfection. The program is a way of life which is very different from the way most of us were operating previously, and it often takes time to make such a radical change. As long as we live, we will probably have to deal with the tendency to be self-centered rather than God-centered. It keeps cropping up and getting us into trouble.

The difference is that we now know what to do when we start to fall apart. We can get back to meetings, call our sponsor and other program friends, and spend more time getting in touch with a Higher Power. A slip does not need to plunge us down into despair. Abstinence is something we are given every minute of every day. We can reach out and receive it at 11:00 a.m. or 4:00 p.m. or 9:30 p.m., even if we have temporarily taken back the problem of compulsive overeating. We now know where the answer is, and with practice we will develop our ability to live this new life.

Most of us find that as we spend more time in the program, the intensity of our problems lessens. There is always room for growth, and as we clear one hurdle, another one usually arises. This may also happen with regard to food — we get the refined sugars out of our life, and we are tempted to binge on cottage cheese. Bingeing on cottage cheese is still compulsive overeating, but the hangover is considerably less severe than the hangover from refined sugar.

What we are aiming for is the ability to put food in its proper place, to eat three measured meals a day with no snacks, and to place every area of our life under God's direction. We would probably never be willing to attempt any of this if there were an easier way to survive. But we find that we cannot maintain abstinence from compulsive overeating (which would kill us sooner or later) unless we are working toward being honest in our relationships with other people, restrained in our demands for material gain, less selfish in expressing sexuality and ambition. The list could go on indefinitely, but this is not just another self-improvement program. The growth comes as we are ready for it, and we do not achieve it by ourselves; our Higher Power gives us only what we can handle one day at a time.

For some reason, some of us seem to have to go backwards for awhile in order to move forward again with renewed vigor. "Taking it back" reminds us graphically and painfully of how miserable the old way is and how much we need to concentrate on applying Step Three in every circumstance.

Surrender

"Take over, H. P. I'm stuck again, and I can't move forward without You. I know You're there. The problem is that I forget to listen. I get swept up in a hurricane of what *I want*. It can destroy me, that I know."

"I want" is very strong. It becomes "I want more and more." Allowed to grow unchecked, it will drive me into insanity or death. I cannot control this "I want" force by willpower, but I can surrender and relinquish it to the God of my understanding. When it comes back, I can turn it over again, every day, many times a day. Each time I turn it over, I am building up the habit of avoiding the self-will trap. Each time I surrender, I am learning to rely on the strength that comes from my Higher Power.

Part of growing up is accepting the fact that we cannot have everything we want. "God, grant me the serenity to accept the things I cannot change, courage to change the things I can, and the wisdom to know the difference." As our will comes into harmony with God's will for us, our lives reflect new confidence, new freedom, and new peace.